DIVING AND SNORKELING GUIDE TO 🐠🐠

Fiji

W. Gregory Brown

Pisces Books™
A division of Gulf Publishing Company
Houston, Texas

Dedication

It is with great love and respect that I dedicate this book to my mother and father. I know they are with me on every dive.

Pisces Books
A division of Gulf Publishing Company
P.O. Box 2608, Houston, Texas 77252-2608

Library of Congress Cataloging-in-Publication Data

Brown, W. Gregory (William Gregory), 1954–
    Diving and snorkeling guide to Fiji / W. Gregory Brown.
        p.   cm.
    Includes index.
    ISBN 1-55992-063-7
    1. Skin diving—Fiji Islands—Guidebooks.   2. Scuba diving—
    Fiji Islands—Guidebooks.   3. Fiji Islands—Guidebooks.   I.
    Title.
    GV840.S78S74   1993
    797.2′3—dc20   92-45216
                                                          CIP

Pisces Books is a trademark of Gulf Publishing Company.

Printed in Hong Kong

10   9   8   7   6   5   4   3   2   1

Table of Contents

Publisher's note: At the time of publication of this book, all the information was determined to be as accurate as possible. However, when you use this guide, new construction may have changed land reference points, weather may have altered reef configurations, and some businesses may no longer be in operation. Your assistance in keeping future editions up-to-date will be greatly appreciated.

Also, please pay particular attention to the diver rating system in this book. Know your limits!

Acknowledgments

I would like to give a very special thank-you to Captain Greg Lawlor and the crew (Sam and Ram) of *Mollie Dean* Cruises. Without their assistance, this guide would not have been possible.

My long-time friend and co-worker, Jeff Talbott deciphered my handwriting and typed the manuscript. For him, this meant long hours and short wages. Many, many thanks, Jeff.

Come to Fiji—it's a whole different kettle of fish!

How to Use this Guide

This guide is intended to give you some relevant information about the Fiji Islands and a good introduction to the types of diving found throughout Fiji. The Fiji Islands encompass a total area of 42,000 square miles, a large majority of which is water. To say there is a lifetime of diving here is indeed a gross understatement. It is simply not possible to cover every facet of the pristine underwater wilderness that awaits. This guide explores only the island groups that are significant to divers. These six groups are Viti Levu/Beqa Island, Kadavu Island/Astrolabe Reef, the Lomativiti Group, the Northern Group, the Mamanucca Group, and the Lau Group. These areas comprise a major portion of Fiji. They also offer the best combination of great diving and accessibility. There are sites in each group that are visited routinely, either by land-based operators or by live-aboards. Of the six island groups, only the Lau and Lomativiti Groups have no land-based dive operations. Fortunately, both groups are visited regularly by live-aboard dive vessels.

This guide includes an overview for each island group. The overview gives general information about the group as well as any useful information concerning the type of diving available. Following each overview is a description of 3-4 dive sites. The sites described are regarded as the consensus favorites. They also happen to be some of my personal favorites. I have tried to include information about the reef topography and to comment on the species of marine life normally found there. I hope this will aid photographers in their selection of camera systems to take on the dive.

The appendix at the back of this guide provides the names, addresses, and phone numbers (where possible) of Fiji's dive operators and information on several of the U.S. dive travel agencies that have years of experience booking Fijian diving vacations.

The Rating System for Divers and Dives

Each dive has received a rating based on skill level. The ratings are novice, intermediate, or advanced.

◀ *Many of Fiji's stunning reefs are characterized by large sea fans and swarms of the brilliant orange anthias basslets.*

One of Fiji's signature species is the colorful soft coral tree, Dendronepthya klunzingeri.

Novice divers should possess a basic scuba certification and should have made from 5-15 dives during the past year. An *intermediate diver* is someone who has received a basic scuba certification and has logged 15-30 dives in the previous year. The *advanced* rating is for those who possess an advanced certification and have made more than 30 dives in the past year. Regardless of skill level, the diver should be in good physical condition and know his or her limitations. Never substitute machismo for common sense.

A couple enjoys a snorkel/swim in the gin-clear waters surrounding Fiji's offshore islands.

Fiji is warm water diving on coral reefs. However, many of the finest sites are subject to moderate currents and lengthy boat rides. Don't expect to step off the beach onto the reef. This is Fiji, not Bonaire.

The diving operators of Fiji often check C-cards and dive logs before letting you on the boat. Following your C-card/log book inspection, the first dive is usually made under the watchful eye of a divemaster. If you perform well underwater, subsequent dives will be less structured. That is, you will be free to plan your own dives.

Note: These diver ratings are loose guidelines, not rigid doctrines. Above all, use common sense before and during the dive. Remember, a buddy team is no better than its weakest member. Make safety the first consideration.

The red or tomato anemonefish, Amphiprion frenatus, *is one of at least four different anemonefish species found throughout the Fiji Islands.*

1

Overview of the Fiji Islands

Geology

The Fiji Islands offer a good example of the various types of islands and reefs that are found throughout the Indo-Pacific Basin. Basically, the islands will fall into one of three categories. The larger, mountainous islands of Fiji such as Viti Levu, Vanua Levu, and Taveuni are volcanic in origin. They characteristically have steep mountains with easily identifiable basaltic outcroppings and river courses that drop precipitously in the higher elevations, often creating spectacular waterfalls. On several of Fiji's volcanic islands it is possible to see the trademark black sand beaches. The smaller, low-elevation islands have a coral (limestone) base. Seldom more than 50 feet above sea level, they are usually ringed with seductive white sand beaches and inviting blue lagoons. These are the islands that perhaps best define the often romanticized South Pacific. Wailangilala in northern Lau is a perfect example of this island type.

The third kind is also an island formed from limestone. Its most prominent feature is a jagged, pitted, irregular limestone shoreline that drops abruptly into the sea. At sea level, this rugged shoreline is often undercut from centuries of wave action, natural weathering, and the scouring effect from chitons. Caves are common on islands like this and they can occur above or below sea level. While this particular kind of island has precipitous bluffs and appears mountainous from sea level, its elevation typically does not exceed several hundred feet. Vanuambalavu, the largest island in northern Lau, is characteristic of this island type.

Thousands of miles of coral reef are found in the Fijian archipelago. The most common form is the barrier reef. As its name suggests, this reef type creates a barrier along the island's coast. Sometimes the barrier will actually encircle the island. This reef usually comes to within a few feet of the surface and it can stretch unbroken for many miles creating an impenetrable "barrier" for navigators. The ocean side of a barrier reef typically drops off quickly into deep water. Sheer coral walls are common on the "outside" of the reef.

The barrier is separated from the island by a comparatively shallow lagoon. At its deepest point, a lagoon will seldom exceed a depth of 200 ft.

Lagoons are often filled with small isolated sections of reef called patch reefs. The lagoons' protected waters (protection is from the barrier reef which absorbs the incoming wave energy) are ideal for the development of delicate hard corals and juvenile reef fishes.

Passages are breaks in the barrier reef where the waters of the lagoon are intermixed with the waters of the open ocean via the tidal cycle. These passages of varying depths are the most productive zones on the reef. Although currents are the norm, passages are among the best dive sites. The combination of colorful soft corals, sea fans, numerous reef creatures, and the larger predators lend an air of unpredictability and excitement to the passage dive. One of the best known barrier reef/lagoon systems in Fiji is Great Astrolabe Reef.

Very similar to the barrier reef is the atoll. The atoll is an irregular "ring" of coral with a lagoon in the center. A true atoll has no central land mass (island). Over a period of geologic time, the island has subsided, gradually slipping beneath the sea.

Simply stated, the atoll is a barrier reef/lagoon system without an island. Navatu, in southern Lau, is an ideal example of a true atoll.

Several seamounts or "banks" are present in Fijian waters. These banks are the tops of underwater mountains that rise close to the surface. They are surrounded on all sides by deep ocean waters and offer prime habitat for big jacks and sharks. The reef development on these subsea mountain peaks is generally poor, but the piscine gatherings can be quite remarkable.

History

The Republic of Fiji covers a vast expanse of the legendary South Pacific. More that 300 islands representing a total land mass of about 7,055 square miles are scattered across 42,000 square miles of blue water. Located between 15–22° south latitude and the longitude between 177° west and 175° east, the Fijis straddle the International Dateline. Although the 180th meridian passes directly through the archipelago, it has been adjusted eastward so that all of Fiji falls into the same time zone.

Lying approximately 1,800 miles east of northern Australia and 1,000 miles north of New Zealand, these remarkable island jewels are bathed in warm, clear, tropical waters making the climate ideal. The mild, dry season runs May–October. Daytime temperatures during this time average 75–80°F with mean evening temperatures at 70–72°F. The warmer season or Fijian summer is November–April. In these months, average daytime temperatures range from 80–85°F. Evening temperatures average 72–75°F. The Fijian summer is the time of year when rainfall and humidity are on the rise. Although rainfall typically comes in the form of a brief shower, these showers can occur quite often during the wettest months of January and February.

Fiji has a total population exceeding 700,000 people. Of this number, approximately 343,000 are native Fijians (Melanesians) and 340,000 are of Indian descent, their ancestors brought to this country by the British during the late nineteenth century to work as indentured servants on the sugar cane plantations. The remaining population (approximately 35,000) contains a diverse mixture of people including Chinese, Polynesians, and expatriots from Australia and New Zealand.

Early settlement of Fiji is believed to have occurred over three thousand years ago (1600 B.C.) by the natives of what is now Papua New Guinea. The Melanesians began establishing more significant settlements some two thousand years later.

One of the earliest known European explorers to wander into Fijian waters was Abel Tasman. In 1643, while searching for new trading opportunities in the southern waters, Tasman came upon a small island just east of Vanua Levu. This island is believed to have been Nukumbasanga. Tasman observed the mountains of Vanua Levu and Taveuni, but chose to head north away from these islands, not wishing to risk navigating around uncharted reefs. Perhaps the thought of encountering unfriendly natives, as he had in New Zealand, was a deterrent as well.

Captain James Cook, a renowned seaman, was also instrumental in Fiji's discovery. In 1774, Cook sailed from Tonga and landed on a tiny island (Vatoa) in southern Lau. He named the land Turtle Island.

While mention is made of Tasman and Cook's discoveries in practically every Fijian history book, there is one man that remains the most famous, or should I say infamous, explorer Fiji has ever known. He is William Bligh, once the captain of a ship called *Bounty*. By all accounts, it was April 1789 when the famed mutiny on the *Bounty* took place. Bligh and some of his loyal followers were forced off the ship into a small, open boat with scant provisions and no weapons. The nearest European settlement known was Timor, located some 4,000 miles away! Bligh knew the long trek to Timor would mean a dangerous journey through the dreaded island archipelago where cannibalism, hostile native warriors, and treacherous reefs were rumored to be commonplace. But he and his crew had no other choice, except slow starvation at sea. Bligh's resulting voyage took him safely through the heart of the Fiji Islands, onward to Timor, and eventually into the history books. It was indeed a miraculous voyage.

Despite continued rumors of cannibalism and terrifying natives, the lure of potential profits from the sandalwood and beche-de-mer (sea urchin) trade drove Europeans to risk venturing farther into the Fiji Islands with greater frequency. Throughout the first half of the nineteenth century, deals were made with several of the island chiefs opening the door for the establishment of viable trading routes across these once taboo waters. Fiji was finally on its way toward becoming a significant part of the civilized world.

On October 10, 1874, the Fiji Islands became a British Crown Colony. They remained a valuable member of the British Empire until declaring their independence in 1970. In October 1987 Fiji abandoned its parliamentary styled government and declared itself a republic, thereby creating a new era of political history that is still unfolding.

At this juncture, Fiji's potential as a world mecca for tourism is finally being realized. In fact, the Fijian economy is now heavily dependent on tourism dollars. Sugar from the countless sugar cane plantations all across Fiji dominate the economic market along with tourism. Other economic interests on the up-swing include timber harvesting, gold mining, coffee-growing, and copra production.

The cane train transports sugar cane, one of Fiji's most important cash crops, along the southern coast of Viti Levu to a nearby processing plant.

A freshwater river courses through the enchanting grounds of the Pacific Harbour Cultural Center located along the southern coast of Viti Levu. The Center is a 45-minute drive from Suva, the capital city.

English is the official language of the Fiji Islands. The Fijian and Hindustani languages are spoken as well. Because nearly everyone speaks English fluently, communications are rarely a problem in Fiji. Believe me, not having to deal with language barriers is a rare treat when you are that far away from home. But then, Fiji has many rare treats for its visitors.

Gorgeous islands, sparkling fish-filled tropical seas, and a wealth of smiling, caring people are all gifts awaiting you in Fiji.

Airlines Service(s)

Getting to Fiji is easy. Three major airlines offer service into Fiji's Nadi International Airport from gateway cities on the west coast of the U.S. and Canada.

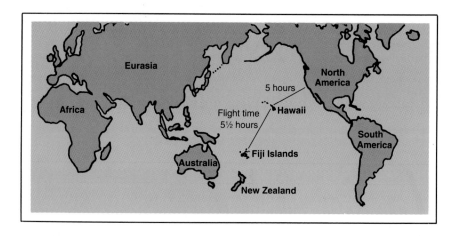

Qantas has three flights weekly out of Los Angeles International Airport (LAX) and three flights per week out of Vancouver International Airport (YVR).

Air New Zealand offers service to Fiji out of LAX four times each week.

Canadian Air (CPAir) has one flight per week out of Vancouver (YVR) and two flights weekly out of Lester B. Pierson International Airport in Toronto.

Although these flights are often termed direct service, they usually have a brief stopover in Honolulu for taking on additional passengers. This Honolulu stopover may entail changing aircraft as well. Other countries offering direct service to Fiji include Australia, Japan, New Zealand, Solomons, Samoa, Tonga, and Vanuatu.

Several airlines are available to transport customers to their desired destination in Fiji. Fiji Air, Air Pacific, Turtle Island Airways, and Sunflower Airlines all have operations working out of Nadi International Airport's domestic terminal.

Ground Transportation

Bus service, taxis, and rental cars are all available, reliable options for ground transport out of Nadi International Airport. While bus service is the least expensive option, it is certainly not without its drawbacks. Often slow, often crowded, and often un-airconditioned, bus travel in Fiji is not something I recommend. Taxis and rental cars are a different matter. For a reasonable fee (prices are negotiable), taxi drivers will take you anywhere on the island. Hiring taxi and driver for the day can be a relatively inexpensive way to get a private island tour at a pace of your choosing. Hertz, Budget, Thrifty, and Avis have offices at Nadi Airport, Suva, and other locations throughout Viti Levu where you can rent everything from sub-compacts to 8–9 passenger mini-buses. Consider the mini-buses a special request item that must be reserved prior to your visit. This reservation can be made and confirmed through your travel agent.

Driving in Fiji is on the left side of the road (British style). The speed limit is 50 kilometers per hour (30 mph) in the city and 80 kilometers per hour (50 mph) on the open highway. Primary roads on Viti Levu are paved and easily navigated. On the secondary roads it becomes necessary to exercise an added measure of caution and common sense. Viti Levu is the only island that offers car rentals.

All you need to operate a rental vehicle in Fiji is your current driver's license and a major credit card.

This traditional style native Fijian hut is known as a bure.

Wrapped in a sulu (a native garment still worn by women and men), this lovely visitor explores a deserted Fijian beach.

Immigration

Once you've arrived, getting into the country is a relatively hassle-free experience. All non-residents entering Fiji must have a current passport that is valid for more than three months from the date of entry and a return or ongoing airline ticket. A visa is not required.

Because Fiji is termed a "healthy country," free from most tropical diseases, no inoculations are required prior to travel.

Hotels and Resorts

A wide variety of accommodations are available throughout the Fiji Islands. They range from international chain hotels to exclusive resorts to small, private guest houses. Most of them offer complete packages including food, entertainment and a full complement of island activities. A list of the available accommodations offering diving and snorkeling are located in the appendix of this guide.

Currency

The Fijian dollar is the primary spending element. At this writing, one U.S. dollar is equivalent to $1.45 Fiji money. Although U.S. currency is taken in most places, prices are usually quoted in Fijian dollars. Any change you receive is likely to be Fiji money as well.

It is wise to exchange an amount of U.S. currency for Fijian dollars upon arrival in the country. What you don't spend can always be changed back prior to your departure (airport departure tax is 10 Fijian dollars—U.S. funds are not accepted).

Credit cards are readily accepted at many of the shops, stores, and restaurants in the larger towns such as Nadi, Sigatoka, Lautoka, and Suva.

Shopping

Most gift shops and handicraft centers are open from 8:00 am to 5:00 pm Monday through Friday and a half day (until noon) on Saturday. Businesses are closed on Sunday.

Handicraft shops are plentiful throughout Viti Levu. The most popular ones are located in the capital city. The Government Handicraft Centre and the Curio and Handicraft Centre are both situated in downtown Suva. They have for sale handmade crafts, trinkets, and beautiful seashells of every size and description. In these "buying centers," there are no fixed prices. It's simply a matter of how much you are willing to pay.

Many divers like to purchase maps or nautical charts of the reefs and islands they have visited. Carpenter's Shipping located in the Neptune House in Suva has a complete set of official nautical charts for sale. While they are rather expensive, it is still a great way to remap and remember your exotic travels in Fiji.

Dining

The Fijian resorts favored by divers offer complete packages including meal plans. In fact, on most islands other than Viti Levu, there are no alternatives to the resort's meal plan. It's the only place around. Fortunately, the food at these "offshore" resorts is typically outstanding. Beautiful reefs and good food are the keys to a diver's heart—and Fijians seem to know this better than anyone.

Naturally, Fiji's multi-cultural population is reflected in its cuisine. From the native Fijians come fresh seafood dishes including their specialty, mahi mahi or wahoo cooked in lolo (coconut cream). The Indian influence is in the form of various curry dishes, mild or spicy. New Zealand's world famous lamb is imported as are many favorite food items of the Aussies. Chinese restaurants are also popular throughout Viti Levu. What you will not find in Fiji is a "fast-food" restaurant.

A phenomenal sunset in paradise marks another perfect end to another perfect day.

After a productive snorkel on the bountiful reefs, there is nothing to compare with a lobster dinner prepared in the traditional Fijian style.

Tipping

Tipping is not a custom in Fiji; however you will find that many restaurants add a 10% gratuity to the final bill.

Exceptions to the "no tipping" custom are the live-aboard crews (divemaster, mate, cooks). Tipping the crew for a job well done at the end of your trip should be an anticipated expense. The amount will vary, depending on the number of crew and divers.

Electricity

Electricity in Fiji is 240 volts, 50 cycles, A.C. This makes transformers a necessity for charging U.S. equipment (strobes, lights, etc.). The wall outlets in Fiji are the European (slanted) style requiring wall plug adapters for the use of any U.S. products. In the resorts that offer diving and on the live-aboards, there are centrally located "charging stations" set up for the guests' convenience. These stations are available to all divers. Everything is ready to use—all you have to do is plug in. Because plug-in space can be limited at these community charging stations, it is wise to pack a power strip in your luggage. Also be sure to mark (I.D.) your equipment distinctively to avoid any mix-ups. If you prefer to charge equipment in your room, be sure to bring a transformer, wall plug adapter(s), and a power strip.

The offshore island resorts and live-aboards generate their own electricity, making high voltage surges a potential problem. To avoid charger damage from these spikes it is helpful to have a power strip with a surge suppressor.

Drinking Water

The water served at restaurants, hotels, and on live-aboards is usually desalinated water. It is pure, refreshing, and quite safe to drink. Should there ever be a question concerning the source of water, simply ask.

The outer reef slopes and passages are often carpeted with spectacular assemblages of soft corals.

From an aerial perspective, the outer drop-off and ring structure of the barrier reef complex is clearly discernable.

2

Diving in the Fiji Islands

Live-Aboard Diving

For the serious diver wishing to see as much of underwater Fiji as is humanly possible in a one- to two-week period, the live-aboard dive vessel is the way to go. It allows you to "eat, drink, and sleep" diving as long as safe diving practices are followed. Four and five dives per day are not unusual among the diving "die-hards" frequenting live-aboards. These dives are often made on the finest reefs and walls Fiji has to offer. (Note: The diving live-aboards currently plying Fijian waters all allow the use of diving computers.)

The long-jawed squirrelfish (Adioryx spinifer) *is one of the family's largest species attaining a length of 18 inches. It is found throughout the islands, always near the shelter of the reef.*

The foot-long blue-striped snapper (Lutjanus kasmira) *is often found in small schools along the outer reef slopes at medium depths.*

Jacks such as these big-eye trevally (Caranx sexfasciatus) *frequent reef passages and offshore seamounts. In these current-driven environments they may school by the hundreds.*

Resort (Land-Based) Diving

There is a wide array of resorts for divers to choose from in the Fiji Islands. The resorts of the main island, Viti Levu, typically contract the services of a nearby dive operation. In contrast, the offshore island resorts are self-contained. That is, they each have their own dive operation. Generally, the dive operations on Viti Levu are a bit more diversified when it comes to services like certification courses, equipment repair, and new gear sales. However, the loss of some services at offshore locations is offset by better diving.

Beach diving (direct offshore access) is comparatively poor throughout the islands. Therefore, the diving at the resorts is almost exclusively from smaller boats (20-40 feet) that take groups to nearby reefs once or twice daily. The standard fare is a one-tank dive in the morning and a one-tank dive in the afternoon. Some dive operations offer all-day diving excursions, but this is usually by special request. In the outer island groups, travel times to the reefs may range from five minutes to one hour. From the resorts of Viti Levu, it takes anywhere from 45 minutes to 2 hours to reach the better dive sites. As a rule of thumb (remember, every rule has exceptions), those individuals prioritizing luxury and amenities over diving may be better served by choosing one of the numerous quality resorts on Viti Levu. If exceptional diving and island scenery are on the list ahead of air-conditioning, room service, shopping, and tennis, then a stay at one of the many offshore resorts is likely to be a better choice.

Equipment

All of the resorts and live-aboards provide tanks and weights for their diving guests. Beyond that, diving gear is not readily available in Fiji. My suggestion is to bring what you need. Although some of the diving operations often rent scuba equipment as well as camera and video, most do not. In some places it may even be difficult to get a weight belt.

Photographers should be aware that items such as sync cords, strobes, replacement parts, and other photographic accessories are rarely available in Fiji. Slide films, an example being the Kodachrome series or Fujichromes's Velvia (both favorites of divers) are also rare commodities. Those lucky enough to find items of this nature will undoubtedly pay dearly for them. What the resorts and live-aboards will have on hand are charging stations for reenergizing strobes and batteries. Because the charging stations are for all of the divers, be sure to I.D. your equipment. Underwater photo equipment can be extremely hard to identify if not clearly marked.

Wetsuits or dive skins are a highly recommended item for diving in Fiji. During the summer season, a dive skin or a one-eighth inch suit will normally provide adequate thermal protection. During the cooler months (July–Sept.), water temperatures can drop as low as 74°F. At this temperature, a one-eighth or one-quarter inch suit is necessary for maximum comfort.

This 10-inch black-spotted puffer (Arothron nigropunctatus) *is being cleaned by a tiny cleaner wrasse. In this picture the wrasse can be seen coming out of the puffer's gill opening.*

Certification

Divers visiting Fiji are usually required to show proof of diving certification, so bring a C-card. If you keep a diver's log, then bring that along as well. Those divers not certified or someone who is new to the sport will have to go through the proper training prior to diving Fiji's incredible reefs. Fortunately, most of the resorts have certified diving instructors on staff. Interested individuals can take a one-day resort course or select a full certification course.

Marine Life

Fiji's underwater bounty is astounding! There are more than 400 species of coral found in Fijian waters. The most spectacular of the corals is the soft coral, *Dendronepthya klunzingeri.* A favorite subject of all underwater photographers, this species is abundant throughout Fiji and it comes in a living rainbow of colors. Its primary habitat is in reef passages or channels where the current is moderate to heavy. There it grows best in deeper water or on the underside of overhangs. The size of an average soft coral of this species in Fiji is only 12 inches; however, the density of soft corals in areas such as Kadavu, Tavenui, or Beqa is tremendous—and precisely why Fiji is called "The Soft Coral Capital of the World."

This 4-inch beauty is the male anthias fairy basslet (A. squammipinnis). *Found on shallow to medium depth reefs with lush coral growth, each male presides over a harem of bright orange females. Should the male die, the dominant female will undergo a sex reversal process, eventually becoming a fully functioning male and the new harem leader.*

The golden damselfish (Amblyglyphododon aureus) *is a small, colorful reef dweller that inhabits steep, outer reef slopes throughout Fiji.*

Aside from the prolific hard and soft corals of Fiji, the numbers of invertebrates found in these waters is too numerous to accurately catalogue (at least no one has done it to date). From flatworms and nudibranchs to octopus and squid to crayfish (lobster) and crabs, the aquatic invertebrate populations are both varied and magnificent.

Because of the vast expanse of ocean encompassing the archipelago, there are subtle differences in the marine community structure from island group to island group. These minor shifts reflect changes in various environmental factors such as currents, food availability, and habitat.

During your Fiji vacation, be sure to make several night dives. It's the best time to find the reef's invertebrates. The nocturnal creatures include hermit crabs, painted crayfish, octopus, shrimp, squid, and shelled molluscs like the magnificent cowries or the poisonous cone snails.

The fish populations in Fiji are among the richest on Earth! Perhaps the signature species for this archipelago are the butterflyfishes and angelfishes. There are more than 35 species of these fishes in Fijian waters. You will observe several species on every dive you make. Among the more beautiful specimens routinely sighted are the latticed butterflyfish (*Chaetodon rafflesi*), saddled butterflyfish (*C. ephippium*), lemonpeel angelfish (*Centropyge flavissimus*), and the emperor angelfish (*Pomacanthus imperator*).

The anemonefishes (often referred to as clownfish) are another popular, photogenic family of fishes found inhabiting Fiji's reefs. They are represented by at least three species in these waters and perhaps five. The

Dive Site Ratings

	Novice Diver	Novice Diver and Instructor/Divemaster	Intermediate Diver	Intermediate Diver and Instructor/Divemaster	Advanced Diver	Advanced Diver and Instructor/Divemaster
Viti Levu/Beqa Island						
1 Caesar's Rocks	x	x	x	x	x	x
2 Side Streets	x	x	x	x	x	x
3 Morgan's Refuge			x	x	x	x
4 Frigate Passage					x	x
Mamanucca Islands						
5 The W	x	x	x	x	x	x
6 The Pinnacle	x	x	x	x	x	x
7 The Supermarket	x	x	x	x	x	x
Kadavu Islands (Astrolabe Reef)						
8 Naingoro Pass			x	x	x	x
9 Usbourne Pass	x	x	x	x	x	x
10 Aquarium #1 and #2	x	x	x	x	x	x
11 North Astrolabe Reef	x	x	x	x	x	x
Lomaiviti Islands						
12 Moturiki Channel			x	x	x	x
13 Wakaya Passage	x	x	x	x	x	x
The Northern Group						
14 Purple Wall			x	x	x	x
15 Mariah's Cove			x	x	x	x
16 Magic Mountain	x	x	x	x	x	x
17 Great White Wall			x	x	x	x
The Northern Lau Group						
18 Boehm Rock	x	x	x	x	x	x
19 Wailangilala Passage					x	x
20 Lewis Bank					x	x
The Southern Lau Group						
21 Navatu Atoll			x	x	x	x

species you will most commonly encounter are the double-bar anemone-fish (*Amphiprion chrysopterus*) and the striped anemonefish (*A. perideraion*).

Other colorful Fijian reef fish you may want to add to your photo collection include the spotfin lionfish (nocturnal), the purple-blotch anthias basslet (deep-water), the fire goby, the coral trout (actually a beautiful grouper), the moorish idol, the endemic, yellow canary blenny, and the long-nose hawkfish. Photograph these and you will have only scratched the surface!

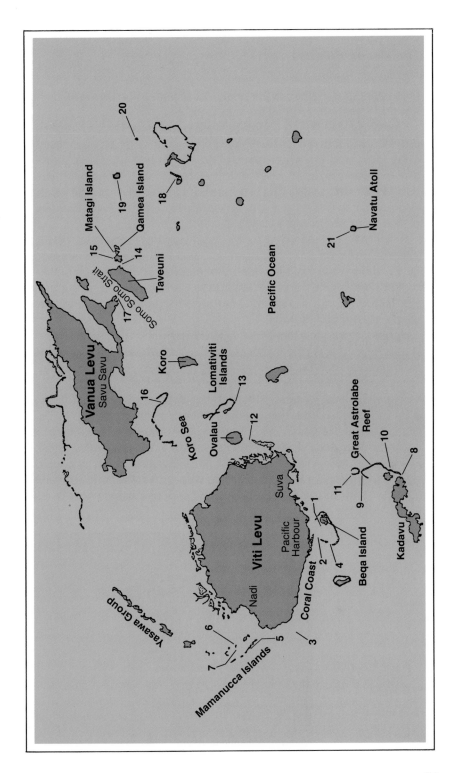

Vanua Levu
Savu Savu

Matagi Island

Qamea Island

19

18

15

14

Taveuni

Somo Somo Strait

17

Navatu Atoll

21

Pacific Ocean

20

Koro

Lomativiti
Islands

13

Koro Sea

16

Ovalau

12

Great Astrolabe
Reef

11

10

9

8

Kadavu

Beqa Island

Suva

1

2

4

Pacific
Harbour

Viti Levu

Nadi

Coral Coast

3

5

7

6

Mamanucca Islands

Yasawa Group

The Diving Climate

Possibly the number one question every scuba enthusiast wants an answer to is, "When is the best time of year to go diving in Fiji?" For this question, there is no easy answer.

Generally, the diving conditions are good from March–December. During January–February, humidity is high and rainfall is abundant. However, the water is warm (82–84°F) and winds are negligible; depending upon whether there are storms in the area, these two months especially can produce either ideal dive conditions or impossible dive conditions. In other words, come to Fiji in January or February and you are rolling the dice.

April–May are regarded as the best boating months in the Fiji Islands. Seas are relatively calm and water temperatures average 80°F. Underwater visibility can be hampered somewhat by plankton blooms, but certainly not enough to warrant canceling your trip. Remember, it is the plankton that attracts gentle giants such as whale sharks and mantas.

June–October are the driest, coolest months in Fiji. Ocean temperatures average 76–78°F but can drop as low as 74°F. If you visit during these months, be sure to bring a full wetsuit. Because rainfall is scarce and plankton levels are down at this time, underwater visibility is at its best. Although the southeast tradewinds are a bit more persistent, they seldom pose a threat to diving. In Fiji, there is always a good "lee" nearby with some excellent diving.

November–December signals the return of warmer water to Fiji. Rainfall increases slightly as do plankton levels. Visibility and wind speed are typically lower compared with previous months. Much like April–May, this period is a popular time for diving and snorkeling.

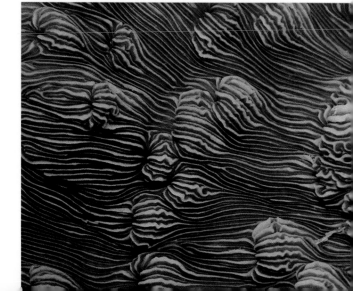

This photo features a close-up look at the artistically patterned porcelain coral (Leptoseris explanata), a member of the hard or stony corals.

This diver glides over a field of staghorn corals in Fiji's northern group.

In the big game category, there are a variety of jacks, barracudas, and sharks. All three of these families of fishes are well represented in Fiji. These larger predators are a thrill to observe and they pose little to no threat to divers, even at close range. Mantas are common in Fiji, while eagle rays and several stingray species are less frequently sighted. The mantas and the eagle rays are often observed feeding in the reef passages when the current is moderate to heavy. The marine mammal population includes pods of bottlenosed dolphins, spinner dolphins, pilot whales, and occasionally, humpback whales migrate through Fiji.

The waters of this region hold a wealth of living treasures. No written words can adequately describe what awaits divers visiting the Fiji Islands. For this reason if for no other, be sure to bring a camera and lots of film.

The Fijian people are keen on protecting their most treasured resource. Therefore, spearfishing is frowned upon and live coral/shell collecting is prohibited.

3

Diving in Viti Levu/Beqa Island

Viti Levu (meaning Great Fiji) is the largest of the Fiji Islands, its land mass totaling some 4,000 square miles. It is home to the westernized capital city Suva, the International Airport at Nadi (pronounced Nan-dee), and it supports the lion's share of Fiji's population. Often called the Big Island, Viti Levu possesses large scenic mountains and rich river valleys. Tourists have numerous sight-seeing options that include everything from multiple-day mountain hikes to white-water rafting to a visit with the families of a traditional Fijian village. The latter is a heart-warming experience you will cherish for many years to come.

Viti Levu is home to approximately 550,000 Fijians. In fact, one of the welcoming characteristics of this island is the delightful people with their friendly nature, warm smiles, and special homespun charm. Equally welcoming is the outstanding diving found throughout the Fijis. But you must know where to look. Like so many Indo-Pacific destinations, the best diving is away from the population centers. In this respect, Viti Levu is no exception. Impacts from deforestation, mining, agriculture, industrial dischargers, and freshwater runoff from several large rivers have taken their toll on the surrounding reefs of Viti Levu. Consequently, the dive operators servicing resorts here usually take their guest to outlying reefs that have, for the most part, escaped the impacts of urbanization.

The most popular offshore destination for dive operators based in Suva and for the resorts along the southern or Coral Coast is the island of Beqa (pronounced Beng-a). Called the "Land of the Firewalkers," Beqa lies only five miles off Viti Levu's southern coast. It offers several sites that justifiably deserve excellent ratings.

Those diving services/resorts based in and around Nadi will make boat runs of 45–75 minutes to access sites in the offshore Mamanucca Island Group.

Although there are a few nice dives along the reefs of Viti Levu, these sites are practically always hampered by reduced visibility and overfishing. They simply cannot compare with the "offshore" reefs.

This lovely broccoli-like soft coral is common around Beqa Island. ▶

24

The exquisite long-nose hawkfish (Oxycirrhites typus) *is a resident at Caesar's Rocks, Beqa.*

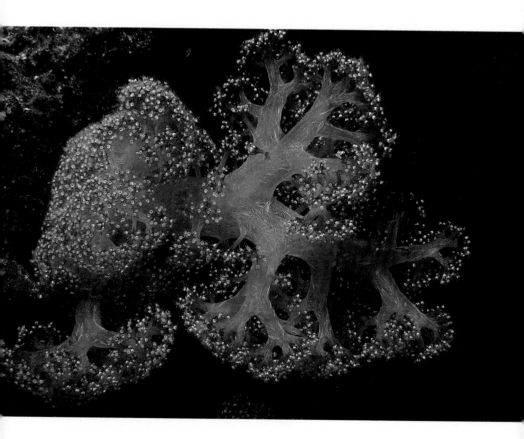

Typical Depth Range:	20–60 feet (6–18 meters)
Current Conditions:	Light–moderate
Expertise Required:	Novice
Access:	Live-aboard and land-based

Located within Beqa's expansive lagoon, the "Rocks" are several coral encrusted spires that begin in deeper water and rise to within 20 feet of the surface. These pinnacles are covered with a wondrous array of small to medium sized marine life. The macro photographer will feel like a kid in a candy store. Sea fans and soft corals are plentiful. Within their colorful branches, tiny gobies, crabs, and brittlestars make unique close-up photo opportunities. Several species of nudibranchs and flatworms are common here as well. Look very closely!

One of these colossal "rocks" has a tunnel through it at a depth of 50 feet. Inside the tunnel are several inquisitive grouper. Each one of them spends some time at the tunnel opening being cleaned by a small wrasse. This is the place to get some nice behavioral photos. The tunnel walls are splashed with multi-colored encrusting sponges and small gorgonian fans. A pair of long-nosed hawkfish dart among the living tapestry.

Because Caesar's Rocks is inside the lagoon, visibility can often be reduced to 20–30 feet. On the positive side, its location usually keeps it protected from surge and wave action. The land-based dive operators out of Suva and Pacific Harbour access this site regularly as does the live-aboard *Beqa Princess* and the boat operated by Mollie Dean Cruises.

Although boldly patterned, this scorpionfish is a master of camouflage. It matches its surroundings perfectly, while it lies motionless in wait of unsuspecting prey.

Side Streets 2

Typical Depth Range:	40–60 feet (12–18 meters)
Current Conditions:	Light–moderate
Expertise Required:	Novice
Access:	Live-aboard and land-based

Situated on the northwest side of Beqa, Side Streets is a maze of coral ridges, caverns, undercuts, and overhangs. This site is located in a passageway, therefore visibility is often a function of the tidal cycle. Typically, the visibility is quite good. One of the travel brochures promoting this site refers to it as legendary. They will certainly get no argument from me. The sea fans come in raspberry red, lemon yellow, and orange orange! The soft corals topple over one another in several places, their colors both varied and intense. Along one of the coral ridges, a field of brilliant orange soft corals highlights the scenery.

The reefs literally pulsate with colorful creatures. Regal angelfish, spotfin lionfish, and numerous ornate butterflyfish are only a minuscule part of the endless parade of marine life that divers will encounter. The thousands of small schooling fishes that inhabit this reef are an irresistible calling card for the larger predators. Consequently, the area is frequented by the fire-engine red coral trout, the white-tipped reef shark, and a few species of scorpionfish whose color will absolutely knock your socks off!

Unusual orange soft corals are found at Side Streets, Beqa.

This is a perfect place for exploration as well as photography. Tunnels, caverns, and caves are prevalent throughout the area. Each one seems to possess a special treasure. Maybe a beautiful cowrie or a sleeping white-tip shark. Anything is possible at Side Streets.

Dive operators from Suva and Pacific Harbour visit this site regularly, as do the live-aboard, *Beqa Princess* and the boat operated by Mollie Dean Cruises.

The spotfin lionfish (Pterois antennata) is an ungainly, yet efficient nocturnal predator. The venomous dorsal spines possessed by lionfish are used for defense and can cause great pain to an unwary diver who blunders into them.

This feisty, 3-inch blue devil damselfish (Chrysiptera cyanea) is aggressive and highly territorial.

Typical Depth Range:	40–100 feet (12–18 meters)
Current Conditions:	Light–moderate
Expertise Required:	Intermediate
Access:	Land-based

Along the southern coast of Viti Levu there is a developed area referred to as the Coral Coast. On the outside of the barrier reef along this section is a site called Morgan's Refuge. It is one of the better sites around Viti Levu. Although it cannot compare to the better offshore sites, it is still a nice dive. The drop-off at this site features some beautiful scarlet sea fans and some colorful tropical species. The deeper depths (60–100 feet) tend to be more interesting than the shallows. Look for the lionfish and a giant Maori wrasse (it is painfully shy) at the 80–90-foot mark. Photogenic invertebrates include flatworms, nudibranchs, and starfish. Visibility is usually in the 30–40 foot range at this site. Sea Sports, Fiji is the dive operator that routinely visits this site.

Several of Beqa's reefs are world-class.

Typical Depth Range:	40–120 feet (12–18 meters)
Current Conditions:	Moderate–heavy
Expertise Required:	Advanced
Access:	Land-based and live-aboard

This site is a large passage located on the southwest corner of Beqa's barrier reef. It has everything expected of a world-class dive site. There are soft corals tumbling over one another in a blazing array of colors. Large colorful sea fans up to 8 feet in diameter are scattered along the drop-off. There are schools of jacks, schools of baitfish, and several gray reef sharks that always patrol this area. The parade of exotic reef fish is extraordinary and seemingly endless. When speaking of this passage, the term underwater photographer's paradise greatly understates the reef's potential. When the visibility and weather cooperate, this area can produce some of Fiji's five-star diving.

During the warmer months, these purple jellyfish are common in many areas surrounding the larger islands.

*The elegant black-spot
lyretail angelfish
(Genicanthus
melanospilus) is a
deep-water resident of
outer reef slopes and
walls. It frequents
depths below 60 feet.
Its maximum length is
only 8–10 inches.*

*A shy, seldom seen resident of Fijian reefs is the white-spotted moray (Gymnothorax
meleagris).*

4

Diving in the Mamanucca Islands

Should you be flying into Fiji's International Airport at Nadi during daylight hours, your first glimpse of Fiji is likely to be the miniature island jewels known as the Mamanuccas Group (pronounced Mamanuthas). These eleven beach-rimmed isles run in a north-westerly direction outward from Viti Levu's western coast. A 15-minute flight from Nadi or a 90-minute boat ride will take you to any one of these tiny pieces of paradise. Ten of the Mamanucca Islands host 11 of Fiji's most popular resorts. The resorts epitomize the South Pacific getaways so often revered by the travel industry. They are enticing, secluded, and romantic, yet maintain all the amenities found at home . . . and then some. With the exception of Malololailai Island, which offers two wonderful properties, Plantation Island Resort and Musket Cove, the other islands harbor one resort each.

Six of the resorts in the Mamanuccas offer scuba diving. They are listed in the appendix at the end of this guide. Most of these resorts have access to the dive sites described for the Mamanuccas. They also visit sites unique to their own resort. The best diving sites typically require a 5–30-minute boat ride across calm seas. The Mamanucca style of diving is relaxed and laid-back. It is well suited for the novice-intermediate diver or snorkeler. The reefs are alive with beautiful tropical fishes and the diving is easy.

A close-up portrait shows how the goggle-eye (Priacanthus hamrur) got its name. It is primarily a nocturnal reef dweller. By day, it can be found hovering motionless under ledges or in the reef recesses.

Typical Depth Range:	40–100 feet (12–30 meters)
Current Conditions:	Light
Expertise Required:	Novice
Access:	Land-based

Due west of the Mamanuccas, the 9-mile-long Malolo Barrier Reef harbors several exceptional dive sites, the most renowned being the W. This section of reef juts out into blue water twice, looking like a giant W from the air. Along the points of the W, a gentle current provides the food base for a wealth of organisms. Pink and purple soft corals flourish under the ledges and overhangs that are characteristic of this site. Also in these areas of low light levels look for the brilliant red fish called the goggle-eye or any one of several species of inquisitive grouper. Away from the reef, out in the deeper water, scan the blue for anything from mantas to dolphins to whale sharks. They have all been sighted here before. More standard fare for this lovely section of reef is the diverse selection of small fishes and invertebrates. Nudibranchs, lobsters, hermit crabs, anemonefish, butterflyfish, and an assortment of gorgeous wrasses can keep photographers busy for an entire vacation. The combination of vivid colors, profuse marine life, and quick access makes the W a hot spot for night diving as well. In fact, the night diving on the reef ranks among Fiji's best. Most of the Mamanucca dive operators have access to this site.

This rather large hermit crab (Dardanus megistos) can attain a length of more than 6 inches. It is a scavenger feeding primarily at night.

This black and white crinoid clings to the underside of a sea fan in the Mamanuccas.

The knobby ocellated nudibranch (Phyllidia ocellata) is primarily nocturnal. Mostly found on inshore reefs and in lagoons, this species feeds on encrusting sponges and algae. It may attain a length of 4 inches.

The Pinnacle 6

Typical Depth Range:	20–60 feet (5–20 meters)
Current Conditions:	Light
Expertise Required:	Novice
Access:	Land-based

The Pinnacle is single coral bommie that rises from an 80-foot bottom to within 20 feet of the surface. It is located just off Mana Island, about a 10 minute boat ride from the resort on Mana. Typical of the Mamanuccas, this isolated coral pinnacle hosts a wide diversity of small tropical fishes from bannerfish to butterflyfish. There are a few orange and yellow gorgonian fans at depths below 40 feet, each one typically harbors a crinoid or two.

This site is protected from rough seas and it is easily accessible, thereby making it an ideal night diving spot. Look for some incredibly colored sleeping parrotfish and some rather sizable hermit crabs. Various nudibranchs are sighted here, too. The dive operators (Aqua Trek) for Mana Island resort access this site regularly.

Schools of tiera batfish (Platax tiera) frequent many of Fiji's offshore reefs like the Supermarket. In most instances, they show no fear of divers.

Typical Depth Range:	30–50 feet (9–18 meters)
Current Conditions:	Light
Expertise Required:	Novice
Access:	Land-based

This shallow reef lies just a short distance from Mana Island. As the name would imply, the reef is loaded with marine life. It has nice hard corals, plenty of reef fishes, and a host of invertebrates. Some of the more interesting inhabitants of this reef are the batfish. They are almost always there and are not the least bit camera shy. But, if you can't find the batfish, don't worry, the resident school of barracudas should take up the photographic slack. The 'cuda move up and down this section of reef, often encircling divers that use good buoyancy control to suspend themselves in midwater above the reef. Have your camera ready and be assured these barracudas are quite harmless.

The hard corals at this site are home to several species of colorful hawkfish. They are the arc-eye, spotted, Forster's, and flame hawkfish. Each one is seemingly more ornate than the other. "Perched" on the coral using their pectoral fins for support these miniature (6 inches long) predators remain motionless until their prey wanders too close. Then with a lightning burst of speed, they swoop down on their intended victim, a juvenile fish or tiny crustacean, devouring it in an instant.

This site is an ideal place to observe the diverse reef life of Fiji. Visit the Supermarket . . . it usually delivers the goods.

The pickhandle barracuda (Sphyraena jello) average 3 feet in length and can be found in schools numbering in the hundreds. They are very inquisitive and will often swim circles around a diver before moving away.

Forster's hawkfish (Paracirrhites forsteri) is commonly located in the shallow water of outer reef slopes. The depth range is from 5–50 feet.

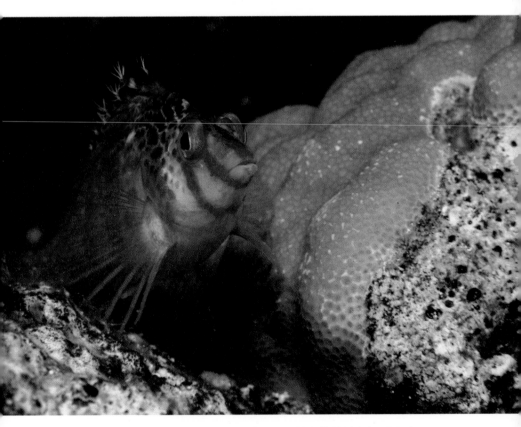

Very shy and seemingly hyperactive, the spotted hawkfish (Cirrhitichthys falco) moves cautiously about the reef in search of its prey.

With a lightning quick strike, this lizardfish has procured its meal, a false cleaner blenny (Aspidontus taeniatus), proving that beneath the thinly disguised veil of beauty, the reef is a place where death can come at any moment.

Kava—A Fijian Tradition

Kava is the national drink of Fiji. The drinking of kava is very ritualized and is long on tradition. It is very important facet of the Fijian lifestyle. Kava is made from the roots of the yaqona tree. The root is put into a large kava bowl and ground into a pulp. Water is then added and the resulting mixture is ready for consumption. Many natives often refer to kava as "grog." Indeed, the grayish, dishwater-like color and its apparent effect on many who consume it make the term grog a most appropriate synonym. The symptoms of kava consumption include a slight numbing of the lips and mouth. Those who drink large quantities often report the onset of a euphoric, narcotized state. Others suggest the euphoria or the "high" derived from kava is nothing more than wishful thinking.

Regardless of its effect, it is used widely throughout the islands, especially when friends gather. Kava is a way of life in Fiji.

Once kava is prepared, the ritual begins. After all the initial greetings, everyone sits around the large Kava bowl. The bowl master will offer you a small bowl of kava. Clap once before accepting the bowl. Then receive the bowl, drink all of the kava, and return the empty bowl to the bowlmaster. After this, everyone claps three times. The next person in the circle will follow the same procedure. Of course, kava drinking occurs amid a party atmosphere. Tales are told and songs are sung and lifelong bonds are cemented together with kava being the glue.

The upside down swimming is characteristic of this coelenterate (Cassiopeia andromeda). It is encountered in the barrier reef lagoons where it rests upside down on the bottom. The free swimming observed here is not commonly seen.

The unicornfish (Naso brevirostris) is a common resident of Fiji's outer reef slopes, walls, and seamounts. Only the male possesses the elongate snout.

5

Diving in the Kadavu Islands (Astrolabe Reef)

The Kadavu Island Group (pronounced Kan-davu) lies less than 60 miles due south of Fiji's capital city Suva. While these pristine islands are close to Fiji's tourism centers in terms of miles, they still remain far removed from the pressures imposed by mankind. Although Kadavu is a comparatively large island, ranking fourth in size in the Fijian archipelago, the total population of the Kadavu group is less than 9,000. In addition to Kadavu, the group includes the islands Ono, Ngaloa, and eight other small uninhabited islets. The natives of these islands lead simple lives that are rich in tradition, virtually unchanged from decades past. For example, before diving around any of these islands it is necessary to obtain verbal permission from the village chief. To accomplish this, a landing party from the dive boat is sent to the local village. A friendly and somewhat festive meeting with the chief ensues, gifts are exchanged, and everyone drinks a bowl of kava. The chief then typically gives the diving entourage his blessing . . . and the diving can commence. Clearly these waters still belong to the Fijian people, and they are highly protective of this valuable fishing resource that has been bestowed upon them.

Very few things have changed in these serene, emerald isles including the mesmerizing beauty of the surrounding coral reefs. At the northern extension of the Kadavu group, a huge barrier known as Great Astrolabe Reef curls around the island chain. Remember the name Astrolabe for it is home to some world-class scuba diving.

The entire western flank of the Astrolabe barrier reef contains numerous channels and passages. Because these openings in the reef structure are situated in the barrier's lee, they offer an exciting calm water starting point for scuba enthusiasts.

This inch-long scarlet fan goby (Bryaninops sp.) escapes detection by predators due to its small size and its ability to blend perfectly with its surroundings. ▶

*The soft coral
formations are
profuse in areas like
the Northern Group.*

Typical Depth Range:	20–130 feet (6–40 meters)
Current Conditions:	Light–moderate
Expertise Required:	Intermediate
Access:	Live-aboard and land-based

Along the northeast corner of Kadavu a passage cuts through the Great Astrolabe Reef complex. It is called Naingoro Pass. Because there is often a moderate current, a drift dive is the recommended procedure for exploring the underwater terrain. The walls of the passage begin in 10 feet of water and slope sharply to the passage floor. The floor then gradually slopes off into deeper water (200+ feet). The passage walls are splashed with a variety of purple and red soft corals. Nudibranchs are quite common in the waters below 50 feet and some magnificent 3-inch long magenta-colored flatworms with yellow trim are often observed at depths below 80 feet. On the passage floor at 155 feet, a couple of soft coral trees, 4 feet tall with a base 1 foot wide stand ready for your wide angle lens. Due to the fine sand that carpets the passage floor, you must approach these giant soft corals from downstream, lest you silt up your own picture by disturbing this easily suspendible sand. Although soft corals, nudibranchs, flatworms, and a full complement of reef fishes present an inviting offering for camera buffs, it is the chance of big game sightings that lures divers to Naingoro Pass. On several occasions large tiger sharks, hammerheads, and sailfish have been observed in this passage. Imagine coming face to face with a 16-foot tiger shark or watching a sailfish streak past you enroute to its dinner. During such encounters, you feel very small, even insignificant—yet very much alive. Believe me, the chiller-thriller experience is unforgettable! As any big game connoisseur is aware, there are no guaranteed sightings of animals such as these; however, the odds are definitely better at Naingoro. Keep your eyes wide open!

The live-aboard operated by Mollie Dean Cruises dives this reef as does the land-based operations on Kadavu.

A diver admires a 10-foot golden sea fan at Usbourne Passage.

◀ *A mated pair of double-bar anemonefish* (Amphiprion chrysopterus) *frolics amid the poisonous tentacles of their host anemone. After a brief acclimation process, the anemonefish are able to prevent their host from discharging its stinging cells (nematocysts). They do this, in part, by covering themselves with the anemone's mucous.*

Typical Depth Range:	20–100 feet (6–30 meters)
Current Conditions:	Light
Expertise Required:	Novice
Access:	Live-aboard

This reef is typical of the diving along Astrolabe's western barrier. On the oceanside of the barrier reef, three coral encrusted pinnacles come within 20 feet of the surface. Healthy hard corals carpet the tops of these pinnacles and aggregations of the brilliantly colored anthias basslets (*Anthias squammipinnis*) seem to electrify the blue water with a bright orange glow. Farther down on the pinnacles' vertical face, huge golden yellow sea fans reach out into the blue and soft corals become more prominent. Bizarre long-nose unicornfish school around the coral heads and wahoo are frequently sighted just off the reef. While it is certainly possible to observe pelagics at Usbourne, the best part of this reef area is the myriad small to medium sized reef fishes that parade by. On either of the pinnacles it is possible to see more than 15 species of butterflyfish. Other species include anemone-fish in their host anemones, parrotfish grazing on the coral, and many inquisitive groupers.

Photographers who don't mind a deeper dive can find numerous burgundy and gold soft coral trees below the 100-foot mark. The live-aboard operated by Mollie Dean Cruises and the land-based operators of Kadavu have access to this reef.

The 4-inch long-nosed filefish (Oxymonacanthus longirostris) is specifically adapted to feed on coral polyps from the angular branches of staghorn corals. It uses these same corals for shelter as well.

Typical Depth Range:	10–60 feet (3–18 meters)
Current Conditions:	None
Expertise Required:	Novice
Access:	Live-aboard and land-based

After Naingoro Pass, the Astrolabe Barrier Reef runs north, away from Kadavu. A couple of miles from Naingoro, this strip of barrier reef has two small blue holes carved out of its shallows. These unique depressions are approximately 180 feet wide with a maximum depth of 130 feet. Very shallow water surrounds the perimeter of both holes. As a result, they can only be accessed during high tides.

Seemingly punched out of the shallow reefs by a giant hole puncher, the Aquarium sites are sheltered from wave action and currents. To a degree, these areas are also free from large predators. Delicate hard coral communities flourish in the protected waters and reef fish of every size and description swim about, unconcerned by a diver's presence. Fields of healthy staghorn corals with pink tips and blue tips line the perimeter's surface waters. Fragile table corals unhampered by wave action grow to gargantuan sizes. Groups of the odd but gorgeous long-nosed filefish feed among the staghorns

Another frequent resident of staghorn corals is the emerald green staghorn damselfish (Amblyglyphododon curacao). One of Fiji's most beautiful damsels, it is typically observed in lagoons (or inside the barrier reef) where it resides amidst stands of staghorn coral.

and schools of colorful flame squirrelfish hang motionless just above the plates of lettuce coral. Reef dwellers such as the exquisite saddled butterflyfish and the golden yellow, blue-eyed lemonpeel angelfish are common residents in the Aquarium(s). In mid-water, a school of gill-raker mackerel are frequently observed straining plankton in unison. If you want to photograph the smaller ornately designed reef fishes in shallow, surge-free waters, this is the place. The live-aboard of Mollie Dean Cruises dives the Aquariums and the local operations at Kadavu visit less frequently.

Massive canyons dwarf the diver at North Astrolabe Reef.

Typical Depth Range:	30–90 feet (6–28 meters)
Current Conditions:	Light
Expertise Required:	Novice
Access:	Live-aboard

This northern-most section of reef lies many miles from Kadavu. It is separated from the larger portion of Astrolabe by the mile-wide D'Urville Channel. In effect, North Astrolabe Reef forms a small atoll that is far removed from the island populace. Upon entering the water, the diver's first observation is likely to be one of scale. The reefs here are colossal structures, dwarfing the human intruder. Massive walls begin at 30–50 feet and plunge into the abysmal depths. Huge, deep ravines divide the wall in many places, providing a haven for species like the tiera batfish or the 5-foot giant Maori wrasse. The reef tops are laden with acre upon acre of pristine hard coral formations and the vertical drop-offs are punctuated with a variety of lacy sea fans. Soft corals are common in the deeper waters where the currents are funneled through the ravines.

A symphony of exotic organisms plays among these wilderness reefs. The secretive flame hawkfish, the uncommon citrus goby, and the endemic canary blenny are merely a sample of North Astrolabe's sizable marine community. Off the wall, out in the blue, anything is possible at North Astrolabe. Humpback whales are sighted every year and divers have been in the water with the incredible white marlin. Mantas are common in these waters as are several species of sharks, including the magnificent hammerhead. Rainbow runner, wahoo, and schools of the delectable yellowfin tuna are also frequent visitors to this area. At North Astrolabe the sea can put on display its finest offerings.

The live-aboard run by Mollie Dean Cruises makes frequent visits to North Astrolabe Reef.

The citrus goby (Gobiodon citrinus) is a shy species rarely observed in Fijian waters. This specimen was photographed at a depth of 30 feet among thick coral growth on North Astrolabe Reef.

Diving in the Lomaiviti Islands

Lying east of Viti Levu and south of Vanua Levu, the Lomaiviti Group is located in the geographic center of Fiji Islands. In fact, Lomaiviti means central Fiji. The group is composed of eight main islands and several smaller ones. The eight islands are Ovalau, Koro, Ngau, Nairai, Makongai, Mbatiki, Wakaya, and Moturiki. These islands are sparsely populated and they harbor no major resorts. Ovalau is generally considered the most significant island in the group because it was the location of Fiji's first capital, a small town called Levuka. Today, Levuka remains a rustic, seaside community, virtually unchanged from 100 years past.

Diving in the Lomaiviti Group is exclusively the domain of Fiji's liveaboard vessels. The favored diving locations are found on the reefs surrounding Wakaya, Moturiki, and Ngau.

This octopus is out at night prowling for a potential meal. The octopus is a common resident of Fijian reefs.

The golden 6-inch canary blenny (Plagiotremus laudandus flavus) *is a member of the sabertooth blennies. It is reportedly endemic to the Fiji Islands.*

Some photos require several dives to the same location to capture a specific creature, behavior, or combination, such as this "mother and child reunion."

Typical Depth Range:	20–60 feet (6–18 meters)
Current Conditions:	Light–moderate
Expertise Required:	Intermediate
Access:	Live-aboard

Approximately four miles east of Viti Levu and two miles south of Ovalu lies the Moturiki Channel. It is frequently used by smaller ships as an entry or exit point through the barrier reef surrounding the eastern side of Viti Levu. This site is, to a small degree, impacted by freshwater runoff from the nearby islands. The runoff tends to reduce visibility, but the nutrient influx coupled with a moderate current seems to stimulate the growth of aquatic life. The concentrations of invertebrates and small marine fishes are quite impressive. There are at least six species of nudibranchs and three species of flatworms commonly observed at this site. One of the photographic favorites is a golden chromodorid nudibranch with purple spots and an electric purple trim around its mantle. As it crawls across the substrate, it periodically flares the colorful mantle, much to the delight of the observant diver. On top of the reef (10–30 feet), divers may encounter the often shy octopus, with its head cautiously poked out of its den while it surveys the reef for a possible conch dinner. The crab population is yet another invertebrate group well represented. Tiny decorator crabs, bizarre hermit crabs, and some large sponge crabs are frequently found scavenging about the reef. The fish population is equally robust and includes schooling anthias, the resplendent ring-tailed cardinal fish, and the delicate, slender pipefish.

Certainly one of the most beautiful members of the Family, the ring-tailed cardinalfish (Apogon aureus) is a shy species that resides close to shelter during daylight hours.

There is not a more wondrous sight in the sea than watching a huge manta ray soar directly overhead. These gentle giants can approach wing tip to wing tip lengths of up to 18 feet. They are harmless plankton feeders that use their cephalic fins to channel plankton into their large mouths.

Typical Depth Range:	40–130 feet (12–40 meters)
Current Conditions:	Light–moderate
Expertise Required:	Novice
Access:	Live-aboard

This passage is located at the southernmost point of Wakaya's small barrier reef. On the lagoon side of the passage, numerous reef fishes such as the lovely purple queen hover atop the hard corals. On the sandy bottom, the wary sentinel goby guards its burrow while its life-long companion, the blind prawn works continuously to keep the burrow free from sand and coral debris. From the shallower lagoon side, the passage floor gradually slopes down to about 90 feet before dropping away into the ocean blue. At the edge

While the sentinel goby stands guard over its home in the sand, the blind prawn (a tiny 2-inch shrimp) keeps the hole free of sand and gravel. The goby and prawn share living quarters in what has to be one of nature's oddest symbiotic relationships.

A green turtle swims toward the open ocean. These marine reptiles are common residents of Fijian Waters.

This little 3-inch blue-spotted puffer (Canthigaster sp.) roams the outer reef slopes during daylight hours. Usually it travels in pairs.

of the passage floor (about 90 feet) a school of resident scalloped hammerhead sharks is routinely encountered by the first divers in the water. These stately 7-foot monarchs are extremely shy, but make no mistake, they are the supreme rulers of this passage. Some other frequent encounters may include massive manta rays, eagle rays, hawksbill turtles, or a thick-bodied jewfish in the 300-lb class. One of the most bizarre sights I have ever witnessed in this passage was a school of 40–60 coronetfish. These strange, elongate creatures are normally solitary predators. The schooling behavior was perhaps for mating purposes.

On either side of the passage, a sheer wall begins at depths averaging 50 feet. The top of the wall has some exquisite table and staghorn coral formations that are teeming with smaller reef species. The face of the wall is spotted with a few nice sea fans and some amazing assemblages of soft corals. When facing toward open ocean, there is one section of the wall to the right of the passage that rivals the best Indo-Pacific sites.

At 90 feet, a garden of 3–4 foot tall burgundy-gold soft corals harbors several lionfish and thousands of 2-inch purple anthias. Just above this showcase, at a depth of 80 feet, the reef has a miniature outcropping that is draped in yellow soft corals. Swarming around this entire area is a school of hundreds of electric blue fusiliers. Below 100 feet, divers will almost certainly observe either the pugnacious bronze whaler shark or the more cautious silvertip whaler. The live-aboards run by Mollie Dean Cruises and the *Nai'a* are the only operations currently diving this site on a regular basis.

7

Diving in the Northern Group

There are over 30 islands in the Northern Group, most of them relatively small. However, the major islands in the group are Vanua Levu and Taveuni, Fiji's second and third largest islands, respectively. While the land mass of the northern islands is significant, the population is rather sparse, numbering about 140,000. The local economies of these islands are driven by agriculture (coconut, paw paw, and sugar cane plantations) and to a lesser degree by tourism.

Several of these islands are noteworthy for their dramatic landscapes. Pristine, white sand beaches with artistically curved coconut palms lie at the base of jungle-clad mountains. The mountain range of Taveuni best exemplifies this geological feature. Rising 4,000 feet above sea level into the clouds, this "paradise mountain" drops precipitously down to the ocean's white sand border. Taveuni is also home to Fiji's most spectacular waterfall. It has a vertical drop of 80 feet and is framed in a post card perfect setting.

If the landscape is characterized as spectacular, then the seacape is nothing short of phenomenal. Fiji is often referred to in the diving community as the "soft coral capital of the world." No doubt, this title was bestowed on Fiji by someone who had been diving in the Northern Group. Colorful soft corals abound in the region. Arguably, Fiji's finest diving is located among these islands. At least two live-aboards frequent this area and several resorts catering to divers are scattered throughout the group. Vanua Levu (at Savu Savu Bay), Taveuni, Qamea, Lauthala, Matagi, and Namena are the northern islands' host diving resorts; each of them is tucked away in an idyllic oceanside setting.

This serene oceanside setting is characteristic of islands in the Northern Group. This is the island of Qamea. ▶

The hawksbill turtle (Eretmochelys imbricata) *frequents remote reefs that are often close to island nesting sites. The hawksbill will feed on items such as jellyfish and sponges.*

Intimidating as it may be, the open mouth of this 6-foot Javan moray (Gymnothorax javanicus) is not a threat response. This particular moray makes its home at the site, Purple Wall.

Typical Depth Range:	35–60 feet (10–18 meters)
Current Conditions:	Strong
Expertise Required:	Intermediate
Access:	Land-based

The Purple Wall is a colorful dive site located in the channel between Taveuni and Qamea. This wondrous wall is covered with purple soft corals, hence its name. The wall begins at 30 feet and drops vertically to about 80 feet. Below this, the reef slope is more gradual and far less interesting.

Typically, this dive begins in a 1-3 knot current, but once you descend below the top of the wall, the current dissipates (actually it is deflected by the reef structure) and you can move about with relative ease. While effortlessly gliding along the scenic wall, it is possible to encounter a wealth of reef fishes and invertebrates. Blue and white chomodorid nudibranchs dot the wall between the field of purple soft corals. Moorish idols and pennant bannerfish are common residents as well. At approximately 60 feet, a 6-foot Javan moray frequents some of the reef's many crevices . . . and it is certainly not camera shy. While not guaranteed, mantas are often sighted and they too seem more than willing to stick around for a few pictures.

Dive operators from Matagi, Qamea, and Taveuni visit this site regularly.

When viewed close-up, the calcium carbonate spicules can easily be seen throughout the body of this red soft coral. These rigid spicules give the body wall support.

The coral reefs of the Somo Somo Strait are laden with colorful soft corals.

Typical Depth Range: 35–80 feet (10–24 meters)
Current Conditions: Moderate
Expertise Required: Intermediate
Access: Land-based

On the northernmost side of Qamea, a small peninsula reaches into the sea. Around the point of this peninsula, just offshore, is a miniature underwater ridge that will capture the imagination of even the most seasoned diver. Beginning at 30 feet, this small wall is literally smothered with soft corals of every conceivable color. They are so thick at this site that it is difficult to notice anything else. The sheer density of soft corals will rock your senses, not to mention the kaleidoscope of colors. The wide-angle photo opportunities are practically limitless. However, it is important to note that the site usually has a moderate to heavy current and these soft corals are very fragile. Therefore, the visiting diver/photographer must be extra careful not to damage to the lush coral growth.

Proceeding into deeper waters (75 feet) the soft coral jungle diminishes and several large sea fans decorate the seascape, along with an occasional reef white-tip shark. This site is visited regularly by Matagi Island Resort divers and Qamea Beach Club divers.

The docile spotted sweetlips (Plectorhynchus sp.) has an appropriate name. It reaches lengths of 2 feet and a weight of up to 12 pounds. The unusual mouth is adapted for feeding on small reef animals such as crustaceans.

Magic Mountain 16

Typical Depth Range:	10–80 feet (3–24 meters)
Current Conditions:	Light
Expertise Required:	Novice
Access:	Live-aboard

The tiny island of Namena lies almost equidistant from the islands of Vanua Levu and Koro. While Namena is small, the barrier reef that encircles it is sizeable with numerous excellent dive sites. One site in particular stands out among the rest. Located in the South Save-a-Tack passage, a coral pinna-

A favorite photographic subject throughout the Fiji Islands is Bennet's butterflyfish (Chaetodon bennetti). *It frequents shallow outer reef slopes.*

This uncommon Randall's sailfin goby (Amblyeleotris randalli) *lives in a sand burrow. Up to 5 inches in length, it often shares its burrow with the blind prawn.*

cle rises from the bottom (85 feet) and comes within 10 feet of the surface. It is an attraction unlike anything Disney could offer and is appropriately named The Magic Mountain. This coral spire is perhaps 75–80 feet in diameter at its base and approximately 50 feet wide at the top.

Various species of hard corals are prevalent on top of the reef. Dense schools of orange anthias basslets flit about in the sunlit shallows as do hundreds of tiny purple baitfish. This congregation of small, delectable fishes, in turn, attracts a host of predators including silvery jacks and the always curious coral trout (grouper), which is a photogenic red with sky blue spots. Several species of butterflyfish in specific pairs spend their entire day feeding on the hard coral polyps in the shallow reef area.

The vertical sides of Magic Mountain are walls of living color decorated with an abundance of dendronephthya soft corals, scarlet sea fans, and black coral trees. The golden damselfish is common along the wall's circumference and the boldly patterned long-nosed hawkfish is a common res-

The extremely wary garden eel (Taenioconger hassi) *is very difficult to approach. This particular species may reach a length of up to 18 inches. It was photographed in a sand channel adjacent to Namena's Magic Mountain.*

ident of the black coral trees and sea fans. Normally deep-water companions, black coral and the long-nosed hawkfish are found here at depths of only 40–50 feet.

At a depth of 40 feet, a large tunnel cuts through the heart of Magic Mountain. This tunnel is festooned with a dizzying assortment of large gorgonian sea fans, soft corals, crinoids, and encrusting sponges, all in a riotous display of colors. It is as if some mad color-crazy artist with a touch of magic had brought to life a favorite painting. Inhabiting the tunnel walls are several species of nudibranchs. Each species is seemingly trying to out-compete the other for color and design awards. A pair of unusual Randall's sailfin gobies can be found at the tunnel entrances; so can a large spotted sweetlips that is usually being "attended" by several cleaner wrasse. Without question, there is a bit of magic in this mountain.

The Magic Mountain is routinely accessed by the live-aboard operated by Mollie Dean Cruises. It can also be dived by operators out of Savu Savu and Namena.

The female blotched fairy basslet (Anthias pleurotaenia) *is a magnificently colored 4-inch species that makes its home on walls and steep reef slopes at depths below 70 feet.*

This unique soft coral is found in dense concentrations below 70 feet on the Great White Wall. This particular color gives off a pale white glow at depth, hence the name Great White Wall.

Typical Depth Range:	40–130 feet (12–40 meters)
Current Conditions:	Moderate–strong
Expertise Required:	Intermediate
Access:	Live-aboard and land-based

The Somo Somo Strait is a narrow stretch of ocean that is funneled between two of Fiji's largest islands, Vanua Levu and Taveuni. Along the southeastern shore of Vanua Levu, an incredibly rich barrier reef is continuously bathed by the current-driven Somo Somo Strait. At one point, the barrier reef juts out into the heart of the strait, coming within two miles of Taveuni's coastline. This section of the reef harbors a site known as the Great White Wall. It is debatably one of the finest dive sites on the planet. The site gets its name from the unique corals that inhabit the vertical face of the wall. Beginning at a depth of 75 feet, "white" soft corals (they are actually a beautiful pale lavender) dominate the wall's seascape down to depths below 220 feet. It is an awesome sight! As the sheer wall plummets into the deep blue, this field of snow white coral seems to exhibit an almost heavenly glow. Despite diving on reefs around the world, it is a spectacle I have observed nowhere else.

The male blotched fairy basslet is perhaps one of the most incredibly colored species found on any coral reef. This one was photographed on the Great White Wall at a depth of 90 feet.

The Great White Wall has many other wonders as well. It is one of the few places in Fiji that has a sizeable population of the exquisite purple blotch basslet (*Anthias pleurotaenia*). These 5-inch beauties sport red-orange bodies, fins trimmed in yellow and blue, and a large day-glow purple square on their sides. By contrast the female of this species is a golden yellow! You will find both male and female on the wall at depths below 70 feet.

The Great White Wall starts at approximately 35 feet. At these shallower depths, there is a profusion of colorful soft corals and exotic marine fishes that will boggle the mind. Butterflyfish, scorpionfish, angelfish, parrotfish, and countless other species compete for your camera's attention. At about 50 feet on top of the reef there is a cave opening. It is wide enough for a diver to swim through. Inside the cave, divers can often observe a lionfish resting upside down on the ceiling. The cave slopes downward and exits on the vertical drop-off at 80 feet. It is yet another wonderful attraction of the Great White Wall. If you ever get a chance to make a night dive on the Great White Wall, DO IT! There is so much indescribable, unbelievable color, and unique night life that you will believe you're floating through a dream world. This site is accessed by the Taveuni dive operators. Live-aboards making regular visits are the *Matagi Princess II,* the boat operated by Mollie Dean Cruises, and the *Nai'a.*

An inviting blue lagoon surrounds a deserted island paradise in Fiji's Lau Group.

This inquisitive coral trout (Cephalopholis miniatus) peers out from under a ledge. The species is commonly encountered on outer reefs in areas of moderate–heavy soft coral growth. Their depth range is 5–60 feet.

8

Diving in the Lau Group

For those who are guided by the pioneering spirit; for those who yearn for high adventure beneath cerulean tropical seas; for those who want to explore some of the planet's most remote coral reefs, a journey to the Lau Group may well be your destiny. Fiji's Lau or Eastern Group is a storybook island chain consisting of more than 50 islands scattered across 10,000 square miles of the inviting Koro Sea. A few of the larger islands are sparsely populated, however, most of the islands are free from the impact of civilization. There are no major hotels here—no prominent resorts—just untold miles of lonely, deserted beaches and magnificent blue lagoons. The Lau Group epitomizes the virgin South Pacific paradise that is often glamorized in the movies. Indeed, these fantasy islands are profoundly magical, extremely sensual, and breathtakingly beautiful. No doubt, the only footprints you will see in the sand are your own.

The underwater world of Lau is the ocean's window to the unexplored. It's quite easy to discover a new dive site. Simply pick a spot and dive. Odds are no one has ever been diving there before. The only changes in the marine environment of Lau are those brought about by natural disturbances. The reefs exist as they did centuries before. In fact, it's quite appropriate to say that diving in Lau means pioneering new frontiers beneath the sea. Because of its sizeable oceanic range, the Lau Group is divided into the northern and southern sections. Northern Lau includes Vanuambalavu, the second largest island in the group. Vanuambalavu is home to a small airport and several small settlements.

Lakeba, in southern Lau, is the largest, most populated island of the group. The political seat of the Lau Group chiefs is located here, giving the island a certain air of importance. Lakeba also hosts a small airport and is home to an elite clan of Fijians who reportedly have the power to call sharks.

The people of Lau make their living by fishing and working on the paw-paw, sugar cane, and copra plantations. Items we take for granted such as electricity, automobiles, and hospitals are things not readily available to them. However, these islanders seem to revel in their tranquil, non-material society. They still understand that family, friends, and faith are the cornerstones of happiness and success.

At this writing, there are no legitimate land-based diving operations in the Lau Group. The only guaranteed way to dive there is by booking passage on the live-aboard run by Mollie Dean Cruises, or by chartering the *Matagi Princess II*.

Boehm Rock <small>18</small>

Typical Depth Range:	20–80 feet (6–24 meters)
Current Conditions:	Light
Expertise Required:	Novice
Access:	Live-aboard

Lying just north of the island of Kanathea in northern Lau, this tiny, fishy seamount rises from the depths to within a few feet of the surface. This extraordinary site is literally inundated with reef fishes. Latticed butterflyfish, anemonefish, hawkfish, colorful sunburst basslets, and several species of wildly patterned wrasses abound. The multicolored crinoids, often referred to as feather stars, are well represented, too. At 50 feet, the walls of the seamount drop vertically into the abyss. In some areas, these limestone walls

This latticed butterflyfish (Chaetodon rafflesii) *was photographed in 30 feet of water at Boehm Rock, Northern Lau Group.*

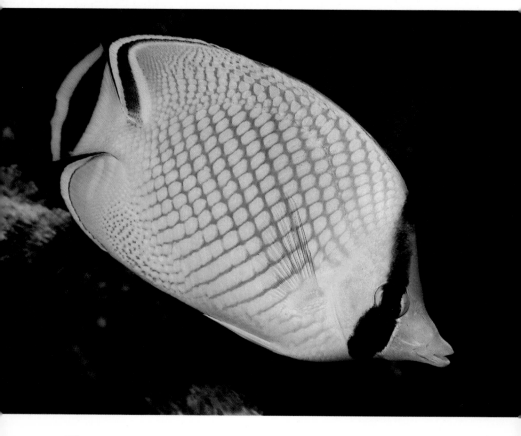

are sharply undercut. Below the overhanging walls scarlet sea whips and lacy gorgonian fans flourish. Perhaps the greatest visual impact for a diver visiting Boehm Rock occurs while diving during the evening hours. In depths greater than 40 feet, as many as 100 of the amazing flashlight fish flit about in the darkness where the seamount's undercut walls are honeycombed with deep holes, cracks, and small crevices. These strange creatures culture luminescent symbiotic bacteria in pouches below their eyes. It's believed that these lights may indirectly aid the fish in performing a number of functions such as food gathering and mating. Divers approaching the wall with their lights on may not get the opportunity to observe this painfully shy, light sensitive species. But those divers extinguishing their lights will be rewarded with one of nature's most spectacular light shows.

Darkness is also an awakening time for many of the reef's invertebrates. Some particularly bizarre shrimp show themselves after hours along the wall's recesses and tiny squat lobsters and decorator crabs can be found crawling on the gorgonian fans.

The sunburst basslet (Serranocirrhitus latus) is a colorful species often observed on reef walls and drop-offs in the Lau Group. Their depth range is 50–100 feet and their primary habitat is ledges and overhangs.

Typical Depth Range:	60–110 feet (18–33 meters)
Typical Current Conditions:	Moderate–strong
Expertise Required:	Advanced
Access:	Live-aboard

At Wailangilala, the northern-most island of Lau, beauty abounds above and below the water's surface. A single passageway cuts through the circular barrier reef of this classic, uninhabited South Pacific isle. This channel through the coral serves as a major feeding ground for pelagics and reef dwellers. The lagoon side of the passage floor begins in 60 feet of water and very gradually slopes down to 110 feet before ending at the ocean-side

This species can be observed along outer reef slopes, in lagoons, and in the reef passages throughout Fiji. The striped anemonefish (Amphiprion perideraion) reaches a maximum length of 5 inches. It is photographed here resting in its host anemone.

drop-off. A drift dive through the passage is the best way to enjoy the endless parade of marine life. The show starts in 70–80 feet of water. Hundreds of small barracudas hang motionless for the wide-angle photographer. On the outskirts of this large school several 150-lb dogtooth tuna do a great job of keeping the 'cudas in tight formation by using the "circle the wagons" approach. At about 90 feet a school of larger barracudas (4–5 feet) will usually come directly toward the diver, passing close by before moving on. But do not put the camera down. There is still a sizeable school of golden trevallies awaiting discovery and 10 or 15 bizarre African pompanos. They will most likely be found toward the ocean-side of the passage at the 100-foot mark. Interspersed among the numerous schooling fishes, divers may encounter several species of sharks including reef whitetips, bronze whalers, and the shy silvertip whaler. There have also been whale shark encounters on the ocean-side of the passage.

Along the passage walls, numerous reef fishes spend their days feeding amid the soft corals. Emperor angels, clown triggers, white-stripe anemonefishes, and the spectacular spotfin lionfish are all photogenic residents of Wailangilala. This smorgasbord of marine life is served to the anxious underwater photographer on a daily basis in an incredible channel only 200 yards long and 75 yards wide.

The live-aboard operated by Mollie Dean Cruises visits this site on all of its Lau trips. The live-aboard *Matagi Princess II* will travel to Wailangilala on request.

A school of golden trevally (Gnathanodon speciosus) *frequents the reef passage at Wailangilala in the Northern Lau Group.*

Lewis Bank 20

Typical Depth Range:	60–90 feet (18–28 meters)
Current Conditions:	Strong
Expertise Required:	Advanced
Access:	Live-aboard

Approximately 12 miles due north of Vanuambalavu lies an open ocean seamount called Lewis Bank. If you like to feel the adrenaline pumping, then

A school of unicornfish swirls across the open ocean seamount, Lewis Bank.

be sure to get in the water here. Visibility is always in excess of 150 feet. That's probably the first thing you'll notice. The second thing will be the sharks! Anywhere from 10–20 pugnacious bronze whaler sharks constantly patrol the area. Within minutes after entering the water these sleek, 3–6 foot beauties will be headed your way, making several inquisitive passes before moving on. Have your camera ready, for they disappear in the blue as quickly as they had arrived. Be assured it's a close encounter of the heart-pounding kind!

This underwater mountain peak rises to within 60 feet of the surface. The top of the mount is covered with small, unimpressive hard corals. The number of reef fish, by contrast, is quite impressive. The lavender spotted lyre-tail grouper and some unusually docile unicornfish are but a couple of the many species that thrive on this isolated seamount. The combination of large predators, colorful reef fish, and clear water are extremely appealing ingredients for underwater photographers.

Don't get so enthralled by Fiji's reefs that you forget to look up every now and then— you might have a manta ray flying over you!

Lewis Bank in the Northern Lau Group is home to dozens of the sleek bronze whalers or as they are more commonly known, gray reef sharks (Carcharhinus amblyrhynchos). Four to seven feet in length, these sharks normally patrol the shadowy depths below 60 feet.

Typical Depth Range:	20–100 feet (6–30 meters)
Current Conditions:	Moderate
Expertise Required:	Intermediate
Access:	Live-aboard

This remote atoll, nestled in the Southern Lau Group, is surrounded by miles and miles of open ocean. It is, by definition, a true atoll. The island that once existed here has long since subsided, leaving only a relatively shallow lagoon ringed by a coral reef. The single passageway through this reef offers the best dive site yet discovered in Southern Lau. Starting in only 20 feet of water, divers will drift through the reef opening toward the open ocean. Once on the outside of the passage, the reef falls away rapidly into deep water. The reefs of Navatu are untouched. There is no fishing and diver visits are rare at best due to the area's extreme isolation, far removed from any populated islands. To dive here is to witness the beauty and bounty of the sea in all its glory, unchanged from centuries past. It is a thrill you must experience.

This massive school of barracuda (Sphyraena obtusata) *resides in the passage of Navatu Atoll, a remote atoll in Fiji's Southern Lau Group.*

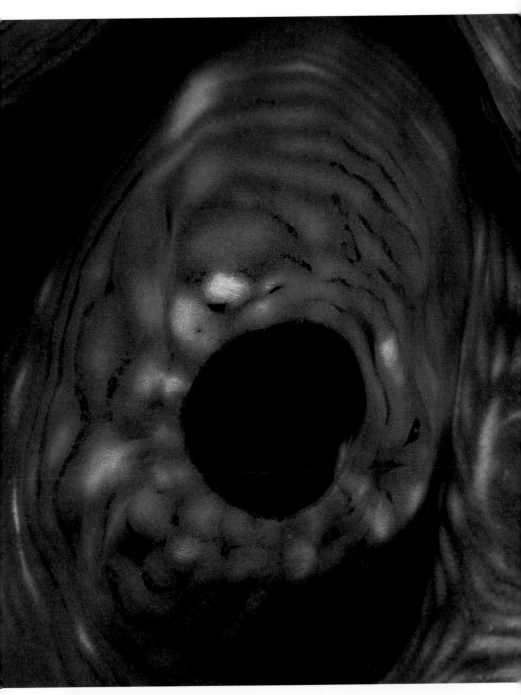

The intensely blue mantle of a tridacna clam is photographed up close showing the specimen's siphon. Tridacnas are common residents of Fiji's shallow reefs and lagoons.

This tropical subsea jungle is rich with wildlife. A mammoth school of barracudas, 300 strong, is always hovering at the mouth of the passage. Directly below them, several bronze whaler sharks patrol the shadowy depths. A large jewfish appearing to weigh in excess of 500 pounds is usually found at a depth of approximately 100 feet. Having no fear of divers, this behemoth can be approached by slow-moving, stealthy photographers. Between 60–100 feet, a large school of big-eye trevallies will often head straight for a diver, then proceed to swim circles around the amazed bubble blower. With the numerous predators occupying these waters, the smaller reef fish are understandably well represented at Navatu.

Inside the lagoon at Navatu, tridacna clams, sporting amazing color schemes, are found among the coral patches, and a diverse community of juvenile reef fish use the protected waters as a nursery.

If a picture is worth a thousand words, then Fiji has an unlimited vocabulary.

Underwater Photography—Keys to Success

There are several essential elements in creating masterful underwater images, and having an intimate knowledge of your subject(s) is certainly one of the keys to success in any form of wildlife photography. This is especially true in the underwater world where the amount of time for taking photographs is, by terrestrial standards, extremely limited. Becoming familiar with a particular organism's habitat or knowing where to observe a specific behavioral sequence dramatically enhances the chance of creating a successful photo opportunity.

Most underwater photographs can be taken using the following lenses: 55mm and 105mm macros for close-up photography; and 15mm, 20mm, and 28mm lenses for wide-angle shots. A single wide-angle strobe can usually provide adequate light for close-up and wide-angle systems.

To master any camera rig requires a great deal of time and effort. There simply are no overnight successes. Lots of practice and hours of careful evaluation are crucial; you must know what your photographic systems can do. But perhaps the hardest part is understanding what the system won't do; that is, knowing the equipment's limitations. (They don't include these limitations in the owner's manual.) Be assured that no one lens does it all.

I make many dives where my sole objective is to photograph one elusive marine species or a specific kind of behavior. Being successful in such endeavors often entails more than a thorough knowledge of subject and equipment. It can also mean multiple dives and long hours underwater at one location. During these sessions, there is no fish chasing, no frantic finning about the reef, and no guarantees—just finding the right habitat, settling in, and waiting for that priceless encounter between subject and photographer to materialize. From the standpoint of photographic productivity, there is, quite naturally, a low success ratio when using this 'waiting game' approach, despite all of the preparation. But frustration dissipates rapidly—for every minute underwater brings new discoveries, fresh perspectives, and unique opportunities. Ultimately, as I have often found, the ocean bears her most precious gifts to those who are patient.

9

Safe, Smart Diving

In Fiji, much of the best diving is found in remote locations, far from modern-day conveniences such as hospitals, emergency air transports, or hyperbaric chambers. This being the case, any diving accidents, especially decompression injuries, have the potential to result in disastrous consequences.

Local Facilities

At this writing, *there is only one recompression chamber in the Fiji Islands.* Keep that in the back of your mind on every dive. The closest available chamber is in Suva. At the onset of any diving emergencies, the first local contact should be EMSEC (Emergency Services Committee). Their phone number is 211-403. To avoid any lapses in communication, it is best to have the local divemaster or dive operator make the call and do the talking. Every dive operation in Fiji should know what steps to take in the event of a diving accident. Every dive vessel should be equipped with an updated medical kit and a breathable supply of oxygen. But it will be up to you to verify this, preferably before you go diving. Victims of embolism or decompression sickness in the Fiji Islands can expect many painful hours to elapse prior to chamber treatment, even under ideal circumstances. Dive sensibly.

DAN

The Divers Alert Network (DAN) is a highly respected membership association dedicated to promoting diving safety worldwide. Its current member enrollment stands at well over 75,000 individuals. For an annual membership fee of $15, DAN offers the availability of diving medical advice and provides valuable information through a comprehensive diver's first aid manual, newsletter, membership card, and tank decals. Any emergency medical advice is initiated by dialing the DAN 24-hour hotline, (919) 684-8111 (collect calls are accepted only in an emergency). All calls that are not pertaining to an actual diving accident or true emergency should be directed to the DAN information and office number, (919) 684-2948 which is available 9 a.m.–5 p.m., Monday through Friday (E.S.T.).

In recent years, DAN has also implemented an insurance program that is available to all divers. This program can provide benefits up to $30,000 for scuba diving accidents. Remember items such as chamber treatments and air rescue transport services can add thousands of dollars to already expensive medical treatments. For further information about DAN write, Divers Alert Network, Box 3823, Duke University Medical Center, Durham, North Carolina 27710.

While there is an organization like DAN to assist divers, it is no substitute for common sense and safe diving practices. Whether using dive tables or a dive computer, ascend slowly and make a safety stop (about 5 minutes) between 10–20 feet at the end of every dive. Avoid decompression dives. Remember, *there are no recompression chambers in Fiji.*

Diver Guidelines for Protecting Reefs

1. Maintain proper buoyancy control, and avoid over-weighting.

2. Use correct weight belt position to stay horizontal, i.e., raise the belt above your waist to elevate your feet/fins, and move it lower toward your hips to lower them.

3. Use your tank position in the backpack as a balance weight, i.e., raise your backpack on the tank to lower your legs, and lower the backpack on the tank to raise your legs.

4. Watch for buoyancy changes during a dive trip. During the first couple of days, you'll probably breathe a little harder and need a bit more weight than the last few days.

5. Be careful about buoyancy loss at depth; the deeper you go the more your wet suit compresses, and the more buoyancy you lose.

6. Photographers must be extra careful. Cameras and equipment affect buoyancy. Changing f-stops, framing a subject, and maintaining position for a photo often conspire to prohibit the ideal "no-touch" approach on a reef. So, when you must use "holdfasts," choose them intelligently.

7. Avoid full leg kicks when working close to the bottom and when leving a photo scene. When you inadvertently kick something, stop kicking! Seems obvious, but some divers either semi-panic or are totally oblivious when they bump something.

8. When swimming in strong currents, be extra careful about leg kicks and handholds.

9. Attach dangling gauges, computer consoles, and octopus regulators. They are like miniature wrecking balls to a reef.

10. Never drop boat anchors onto a coral reef.

The pennant bannerfish (Heniochus chrysostomus) is a gorgeous specimen attaining a length of 6 inches. It usually inhabits areas of heavy hard coral growth at depths between 10–60 feet. It is typically found in pairs.

Appendix: Dive Services

This information is included as a service to the reader. The author has made every effort to make this list accurate at the time the book was printed. This list does not constitute an endorsement of these operators and dive shops. If operators/owners wish to be considered for future reprints/editions, please contact Pisces Books, P.O. Box 2608, Houston, Texas 77252-2608.

Mamanucca Group/Viti Levu (Nadi Area)

Subsurface Fiji Ltd.
P.O. Box 364
Lautoka, Fiji
Tel: (679) 661500
Fax: (679) 664496

Elegant Divers/Tokoriki Island Resort
P.O. Box 718
Nadi, Fiji
Tel: (679) 661999
Fax: (679) 665295

Mamanucca Divers
Musket Cove Resort
Private Mail Bag
Nadi Airport, Fiji
Tel: (679) 662215
Fax: (679) 662633

Mana Island Resort/Aqua Trek
P.O. Box 610
Lautoka, Fiji
Tel: (679) 661455
Fax: (679) 780412

Plantation Island Divers
Plantation Island Resort
P.O. Box 9176
Nadi, Fiji
Tel: (679) 722333
Fax: (679) 790163

Seashell Cove Dive Shop/H₂O Sportz
P.O. Box 9530
Nadi Airport, Fiji
Tel: (679) 790100
Fax: (679) 790294

Sheraton Fiji Resorts/Tropical Divers
P.O. Box 9063
Nadi Airport, Fiji
Tel: (679) 723435
Fax: (679) 701818

South Sea Divers/Aqua Trek
P.O. Box 10215
Nadi, Fiji
Tel: (679) 780413
Fax: (679) 780412

Viti Levu (Coral Coast and Suva)/Beqa Island

Beqa Divers Fiji
GPO Box 777
Suva, Fiji
Tel: (679) 361088 24 hours
Fax: (679) 361047

Dive Connection
P.O. Box 14869
Suva, Fiji
Tel: (679) 450371
Fax: (679) 450371

Marlin Bay Resort
P.O. Box 112
Pacific Harbour, Fiji
Tel: (679) 304042
Fax: (679) 304028

Ocean Pacific Divers
P.O. Box 3229
Lami, Fiji
Tel: (679) 303252
Fax: (679) 361577

Sea Sports Ltd.
P.O. Box 688
Sigatoka, Fiji
Tel: (679) 50225 or 50598
Fax: (679) 520239

Astrolabe Reef/Kadavu Island

Astrolabe Divers
c/o P.O. Nagara
Kadavu, Fiji
Tel: (679) 302689
Fax: (679) 302689

Malawai Bay
P.O. Box 1277
Suva, Fiji
Tel: (679) 361-977
Fax: (679) 361536

Mantana Resort
P.O. Box 8, Vunisea
Kadavu, Fiji
Tel: (679) 311780
Fax: (679) 303860

Northern Group

Curliz/Sea Fiji
P.O. Box Savusavu
Fiji
Tel: (800) 854-3454
Fax: (679) 850345

Dive Taveuni
P.O. Box Matei
Taveuni, Fiji
Tel: (679) 880441 or 880445
Tel: (800)-FORBES-5
Fax: (679) 880466

Forbes Laucala Island
P.O. Box 41 Waiyevo
Taveuni, Fiji
Tel: (679) 880077
Fax: (679) 880099
or (800) FORBES5
US# (719) 379-3263

Garden Island Resort Divecentre
P.O. Box 1, Waiyevo
Taveuni, Fiji
Tel: (679) 880286
Fax: (679) 880288

H$_2$O Sportz
Nakoro Resort
P.O. Savusavu
Fiji
Tel: (679) 850156
Fax: (679) 850340

Konitiki Resorts
c/o Gemini Pacific Corp.
P.O. Box 51
Pacific Harbour Deuba
Fiji
Tel: (679) 850262
Fax: (679) 850355

Matagi Island Resort
P.O. Box 83, Waiyevo
Taveuni, Fiji
Tel: (679) 880260
Fax: (679) 880274
US (800)-3-MATAGI

Moody Namenalala Resort
Private Mail Bag
Savusavu, Fiji
Tel: (679) 813764

Namale Plantation Resort
P.O. Box 244
Savusavu, Fiji
Tel: (679) 850435
Fax: (679) 850400

Qamea Beach Club
P.O. Matei
Taveuni, Fiji
Tel: (800) 447-8999
Tel CA: (213) 546-1447

Live-Aboard Boats

Beqa Princess
Dive Connections
P.O. Box 14869
Suva, Fiji
Tel: (679) 450371
Fax: (679) 450371

Matagi Princess II
Tropical Dive Enterprises
P.O. Box 83, Waiyevo
Taveuni, Fiji
Tel: (679) 880260-301780
Fax: (679) 880274
1-800-3-MATAGI

Mollie Dean Cruises
P.O. Box 3256
Lami, Fiji
Tel: (679) 361652
Fax: (679) 361137

Nai'a
See & Sea Travel
50 Francisco St. #205
San Francisco, CA 94133
Tel: (415) 434-3400
Fax: (415) 434-3409

U.S. Dive Travel Agents

These agents have experience booking dive travel in the Fiji Islands.

Adventure Express
650 Fifth St., Suite 505
San Francisco, CA 94107
Tel: (800) 443-0799
(415) 442-0799
Fax: (415) 442-0289

Aqua Trek
110 Sutter St., Suite 811
San Francisco, CA 94104
Tel: (800) 541-4334
(415) 398-8990
Fax: (415) 398-0479

I.D.E.
11360 Matinicus Ct.
Cypress, CA 90630
Tel: (800) 544-3483
Fax: (714) 891-2154

Poseidon Ventures
359 San Miguel Drive
Newport Beach, CA 92660
Tel: (800) 854-9334

Sea Safaris
3770 Highland Ave., Suite 102
Manhattan Beach, CA 90266
Tel: (800) 821-6670
(800) 262-6670 CA only
Fax: (213) 546-2464

See and Sea Travel Service
50 Francisco St., Suite 205
San Francisco, CA 94133
Tel: (800) 348-9778
(415) 434-3400
Fax: (415) 434-3409

Tropical Adventures Travel
111 Second North
Seattle, WA 98109
Tel: (800) 247-3483
(206) 441-3483
Fax: (206) 441-5431

Index